About the Book

When Young Will Cody walked into the stockade at Fort Leavenworth, he saw Indians of every tribe, scouts in fringed jackets and soldiers on horses. This was the world of the Wild West, so different from Iowa, where he had lived as a small boy.

Will, known to the world as Buffalo Bill, later rode for the pony express and wagon trains, traveling through unexplored and dangerous territories. He scouted for the Union Army, often in the harshest conditions. His bravery and great adventures, most of which occurred before he was twenty-five, made him a legend in his own lifetime.

When the Wild West was gone, Buffalo Bill's Wild West Shows were keeping it alive. The West lived again as people the world over watched on.

W · F · COD

BUFFALO BILL

by Eden Vale Stevens
drawings by Joseph Ciardiello

G.P. Putnam's Sons   New York

Text copyright © 1976 by Eden Vale Stevens
Illustrations copyright © 1976 by Joseph Ciardiello
All rights reserved. Published simultaneously in Canada
by Longman Canada Limited, Toronto.
Printed in the United States of America
06209
Library of Congress Cataloging in Publication Data
1. Cody, William Frederick, 1846-1917—Juvenile
literature.   [1. Cody, William Frederick, 1846-1917.
2. The West—Biography]
I. Ciardiello, Joseph.   II. Title.
F594.C6875 1976 978'.02'0924 [B] [92] 75-26514
ISBN 0-399-20493-8 ISBN 0-399-60983-0 lib. bdg.

For Tony

Young Will Cody climbed up on the big wagon beside his father. The Cody family was leaving Le Claire, Iowa, and heading west for Kansas. The wagon was full of their belongings and the things they would try to trade to the Indians.

Some months before, Will's older brother, Samuel, had been killed in a fall from a horse. His mother was so sad that Will's father decided to sell the farm and their animals and move to a new home.

From the high wagon seat Will
looked back at the places where
he and his brother and two sisters
had played. He looked at the gray
wooden house in which he had
been born eight years before, on
February 26, 1846.

Now it was time to leave.

"Take tight hold of the reins,"
Isaac Cody reminded his son.
Will, who loved horses and riding, was just learning to drive the
four horses that pulled the wagon.

Will touched the whip to the
back of the lead horse. The wagon
picked up speed. They were on
their way. Will and his father began to sing.

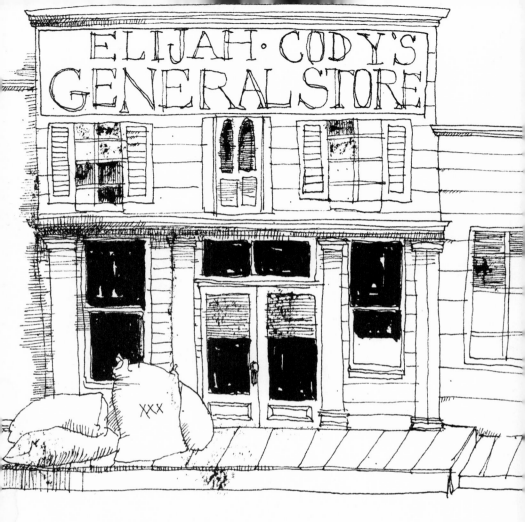

The Codys' journey lasted
thirty days. At last, dusty and
tired, they arrived at Weston, Missouri, on the border of Kansas.

Will's Uncle Elijah lived there and ran a general store.

Uncle Elijah put their belongings into one of his storehouses and gave the Codys a place to stay until they could find a home of their own in Kansas.

On their first trip into Kansas Will and his father crossed the Missouri River. They stopped at Fort Leavenworth. Will had never seen a stockade before. Everything interested him. But Will liked the soldiers on horses—the cavalry—best.

Will saw Indians of many tribes there—Kickapoo, Arapaho, Delaware, Choctaw, and others. He

made friends with a boy of the Kickapoo tribe. Will saw men in buckskin shirts and wide-brimmed hats. These were the scouts who rode ahead of the cavalry looking for campsites and spying out danger.

One fine day Will and his father climbed to the top of a hill. They looked out over the rolling grasslands of the Salt Creek Valley. Isaac Cody decided to build their new home on this land.

The next morning Will's father began to trade blankets and beads to the Indians for horses. One of the first trades was a wild pony, which he gave to Will. "He's yours, son," Mr. Cody said, "but you'll have to break him yourself." This meant that Will would have to train the pony.

Will named the pony Prince. He trained him with firmness and kindness, until he could ride him.

Kansas was not yet a state, but a territory. The land the Codys settled lay between the Southern states and the Northern states. The South allowed slavery, and the North did not. When a law was passed in Washington allowing the territories to vote on the issue of slavery, people from both the North and the South began pouring in to claim the land, each for his own side. Heated arguments over the question of slavery often led to fights.

One night Will and his father went to the store to buy feed for the horses. Isaac Cody promised his wife not to talk politics with anyone. She was afraid of his getting into a fight. But as Will and his father passed a group of loud-talking men, one of them shouted, "Cody, where do you stand?"

Isaac Cody moved quickly through the crowd, jumped up on a box, and made a speech that ended with the words "I'm against slavery!"

"Get off that box, or I'll knock you off!" a man yelled.

Another pulled out a knife and stabbed Will's father in the back.

A neighbor carried Isaac Cody into his house. Young Will rode off to fetch his mother.

A time of hardship began for the Codys. Will's wounded father had to hide in the fields because the proslavery men were after him. At night Will and his sister Julia brought him food and medicine.

In 1854 an election was held to see whether the territory of Kansas should be for or against slavery when it entered the Union. The proslavery men won. The fighting became even more furious. Each side was now determined to make Kansas go its way when statehood was won. Once Kansas became a state, a final election, deciding for or against slavery would be held.

Isaac Cody fled thirty-five miles west of Leavenworth, where he thought he would be safe. Will and the rest of the family stayed behind. Mr. Cody started a sawmill.

One night Mrs. Cody found out his enemies knew where her husband was hiding and were planning to kill him. She sent Will to warn his father. Will set out on Prince but ran into a gang of these men. He got away. The men followed, but Will and his pony were too fast for them and he warned his father in time.

Mr. Cody returned home one night. The men came looking for him. He hid in the attic. Will and Julia sat in the dark on the top rung of the attic ladder with a shotgun over their knees to protect their father. When the men left, they took Prince with them.

During the winter the Codys nearly starved. Mr. Cody had no money to send his family. His sawmill had failed. In April Isaac Cody died.

Gold had been discovered in California. Thousands of men, women, and children, some on foot, some on horseback, and some in covered wagons streamed past the Codys' door. The Gold

Rush was on. Everyone wanted to go west and strike it rich. Will wanted to go, too. But his family needed him.

Will had to earn money. He begged his mother to let him go to work for Alexander Majors, whose wagons, pulled by mules, carried supplies and mail to the westward travelers.

Will's mother asked Mr. Majors to give Will a job as a messenger.

"There are Indians and robbers and rattlesnakes along the way. The job is dangerous," Mr. Majors said. "Will is too young."

"I can ride as well as any man," Will said. "And shoot as well, too."

Will was ten years old when Mr. Majors gave him the job. Will received forty dollars a month and his food. The money was paid to his mother.

Will's next job, that same year, was with a wagon train taking supplies to Salt Lake City. Will rode a mule and herded the extra cattle.

Once outlaws attacked the wagon train, capturing the cattle and guns. They set fire to the wagons. Will and the others had to walk the thousand miles home.

In the spring Will had a horse, instead of a mule, to ride. The wagon train stopped at Old Fort Laramie. Here Will met the famous scouts Kit Carson and Jim Bridger. He sat for hours and watched these men talk to the Indians in sign language, which he tried to learn. He also began to learn the Sioux language. Will Cody had decided to become a scout.

Will practiced writing his name. He printed it on wagons and canvas with a burnt stick. He carved it with a knife on wood. He was twelve years old, but there had been little time for school.

When he was paid, he went home and spread the big silver dollars out on the table. It made Will proud to be able to help his family.

Will decided to try fur trapping and trading. He and a friend Dave bought two oxen, a wagon, and supplies and set out for the Rocky Mountains.

About two hundred miles from home they found a good place to camp. They built a dugout in the side of the mountain, roofing it with branches, long grass, and earth. They started to trap.

A grizzly bear wandered into their camp and killed the oxen.

Two days later Will cut his leg.

Dave went off to get help, leaving
Will alone in the dugout. Indians
came down and carried off the

furs and some of the food. They spared Will's life because he had made friends with a son of one of the braves at Fort Leavenworth.

Snowed in, with wolves howling around the dugout, Will waited twenty-one days before Dave came back to rescue him.

Next, Will got a job with Alf Slade riding for the pony express. Some Indians had been attacking their stagecoaches and stealing horses. When Mr. Slade and a

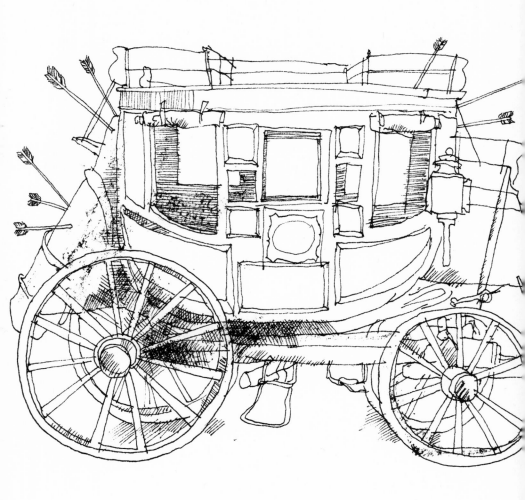

party of men went looking for them, Will went along.

Wild Bill Hickok led the party. When they tracked down the Indians, the Slade Party was outnumbered four to one. But Wild Bill, who was afraid of nothing and was the best rider in the West, hid behind a rock until the Indians were asleep. He rounded up the stolen horses. Then Wild Bill rode around and around the Indian camp, yelling and shooting like a wild man. The Indians thought they were surrounded, and Mr. Slade and Will and all the others got safely away with the horses.

Wild Bill Hickok was ten years older than Will. He was the bravest man and the best shot Will had ever known. Will tried to be like him. The two became friends and remained so all their lives.

In 1861 Kansas was admitted to the Union. There was a new election to decide whether the state would be free or proslavery. This time the men for freedom won. But the men who were for slavery were so angry to have lost they fought harder than ever. They burned and killed. Kansas became known as Bloody Kansas, but it remained a free state.

All over the nation, the argument about slavery went on and on. President Abraham Lincoln did his best to keep the Union strong, but the nation was divided. In the same year—1861— the Civil War began.

Will Cody was only fifteen, but he wanted to fight for the Union and the right of every person to be free. His mother begged him to stay home to help his family. Will took a job driving a team of horses, but because he was such a fine rider, he sometimes carried messages for the Union Army.

Then Will's mother died. He had to work harder than ever to support his sisters and little brother.

When Will's sister Julia married, she took the younger children to live with her. Will could now enlist in the Army.

It was the year 1864. Will was eighteen.

Private Cody served as a scout and at times as a spy in the Southern territories. Dressed as a farm boy and riding a farm horse, he got through the Confederate Army lines. He found out where

the enemy troops were, then rode
back to his side to report.

Later Will was stationed in St.
Louis, Missouri. One day he saw

a girl being frightened by some drunken soldiers. Will fought the soldiers and drove them away. The girl's name was Louisa Frederici.

Two years later Louisa and Will were married. Will was twenty-two years old. His hair hung to his shoulders, and he had started to grow a mustache and a goatee. He dressed in a fringed buckskin jacket and a red shirt. He was already famous as a scout, a quick shot, a fine horseman, and a stage-coach driver who could outwit robbers and fight Indians. But he had no job.

Will tried to become a business-
man. He ran a hotel which he
called the Golden Rule Hotel. It

was very popular, but it made no money because Will gave almost everything away free.

Then Will tried to make money selling land. He started a town on the prairie where the trains stopped. He called the town Rome. He was proud of his town, and he went to get his wife Louisa. When Louisa and Will arrived in Rome, the railroad had moved, and all the people with it.

The Civil War was over, but now the Army was ordered to fight the Indians. The government had broken many treaties with the Indians and had taken their lands. The hunting grounds were being destroyed. The Indians were fighting for their rights.

General George Custer came from the East to fight the Indians. Will became a scout for him.

Later Will scouted for the Tenth Cavalry, an all-black regiment.

After this, Will took the job of supplying buffalo meat to a great railway company. With his horse,

General Custer

Brigham, and his old gun he called Lucrecia Borgia, Will became the champion buffalo hunter of the West. He earned the nickname Buffalo Bill.

Men talked about Buffalo Bill around their campfires. Newspapers everywhere told of his deeds. Stories, books, and plays were written about him.

Buffalo Bill hunted thousands of wild buffalo, but he did so to supply a need. Every day he risked his life to provide the food needed by the men who were laying the railroad track across the vast prairie.

He fought Indians, but he always fought fair. After the Indian wars, many Indian chiefs became his friends. Sitting Bull, Medicine Horse, Hard to Hit, One Star—all knew that when Pahaska, as they called Buffalo Bill, gave his word, he kept it.

One of Buffalo Bill's last scouting jobs was for General Hazen of the United States Cavalry. He rode three hundred and fifty miles in less than sixty hours to deliver an important message. For this he was made Chief of Scouts.

By 1871 the railroad was carrying passengers and freight from coast to coast. Telegraph wires

hummed with messages. Buffalo Bill was twenty-six years old. He had won the Congressional Medal of Honor. He had been elected to the Nebraska legislature. Everyone admired him. But once again, he was out of work.

One day a man called Ned Buntline, who had written many books about Buffalo Bill, came looking for him. He found him under a wagon, asleep. This was the beginning of a new life for Buffalo Bill.

Ned Buntline took him to New York City. Buffalo Bill acted in a play called *Scout of the Plains*, playing himself. The audience loved him.

Everyone wanted to meet him. He wore fine clothes and went to many parties. He earned a great deal of money and bought a big house in Rochester, New York, for his wife, Louisa, and his daughters, Ora and Arta, and his little son, Kit Carson Cody.

Buffalo Bill decided to start a Wild West Show. In towns all over America he rented large spaces to put on his show. Scouts and cowboys rode once more. Chief Sitting Bull and other great chiefs brought their braves, their wives, and their children to take part. With guns shooting into the air and cries and shrieks, once again the old stagecoach was attacked. Once again robbers held up the pony express and the Indian fought the white man.

It was all make-believe.

The people watched Buffalo Bill on his beautiful horse, his

long hair flowing over his shoulders. Wearing a Stetson hat, a fringed leather jacket, and high-heeled boots, he rode as only Buffalo Bill could ride.

Until he died in 1917, Buffalo Bill was the star of his Wild West Show. He took his show with its hundreds of animals and performers all over the world. The Old West was gone. But for presidents and kings and queens and the children of many lands, Buffalo Bill made it live again.

About the Author

EDEN VALE STEVENS was brought up in northern Minnesota. She has contributed to many magazines, including *Mademoiselle, McCall's, Ladies' Home Journal,* and *Scholastic.*

Mrs. Stevens has also written two books, *Abba* and *The Piper,* as well as two operas, plays, and numerous stories for the Children's Theatre in Rockland County, New York, of which she is both director and producer.

About the Artist

JOSEPH CIARDIELLO studied at the High School of Art and Design, Parsons School of Design, and the New School in New York City.

His illustrations have appeared in numerous national publications, among them *New Times, Crawdaddy, Penthouse, Genesis, Practical Psychology,* and *Scholastic.*

Mr. Ciardiello's work has been in several exhibitions, including the Society of Illustrators' Annual Exhibition.

Mr. Ciardiello's talents are not restricted to art — he is also a fine musician. This is his first book for children.